Sound in Film

The Change from Silent Film to the Talkies

By

Allardyce Nicoll

British Library Cataloguing-in-Publication Data
A catalogue record for this book is available from
the British Library

THE SOUND FILM

WHEN sound was first added to the silent forms presented in the cinema, a great outcry arose from those intellectuals who had up to then sponsored and supported the new art, as well as from a number of directors who, aiming more highly than others, felt that they were rapidly mastering the secrets of this medium. Pudovkin at first stoutly opposed the introduction of sound on aesthetic grounds. Writing in 1930 Paul Rotha, likewise condemning reproduction of the human voice, declared that he was

> certain that these new forms will never destroy the original and highest form of cinema, the silent, flat film with synchronised or orchestra accompaniment, which is indisputably the most effective medium for the conveyance of the dramatic content of a theme to the mind of an audience.

This judgment he repeated in his next book (1931), where he averred that, although "sound can help the cinema as a means of expression," "speech is proving detrimental to it"; Chaplin he praised because "from the time when the recorded voice was first employed in conjunction with screen images" that actor had "observed the futility of the attempt."

J. G. Fletcher in 1929 categorically dismissed the possibilities which might reside in the combination of visual and audible elements:

A complete boycott of "talking films" should be the first duty of anyone who has ever achieved a moment's pleasure from the contemplation of any film

expressed clearly his point of view. In the same year Katharine Gerould declared that, if the talkies prevailed, "then the art of the motion-picture, with its immense possibilities, will be in our own generation as 'lost' as the Egyptian art of embalming."

These judgments were written only a few years ago; but Time has many revenges. Time, even the short time that has elapsed between 1926 and the present, has demonstrated the falsity at least of such prognostications as are embodied in Rotha's words and seems to have gone further towards a disproving of the aesthetic standards implied in Fletcher's appeal. The sound film has fully established itself in the esteem of the public; by no possible imagining can we credit the return to favour of the silent film; and recent years have shown such a marked advance in the former's artistic excellence that we believe it to contain potentialities far in advance of anything achieved or even imagined ten years ago.

That popular success in itself does not imply, of course, the most artistic choice needs no special emphasis. The public has shown itself at fault in the past, and indeed there are many still who deplore the loss of good old days, haloed with the light of fond recollection, when no voice proceeded from the silent expanse of the screen. Of necessity, we must consider the validity of their position, and, in order to accomplish this task impartially, we are compelled to make several admissions.

EFFECTS OF SOUND

When Al Jolson came forward with *The Jazz Singer* and *The Singing Fool* a monkey wrench unquestionably was firmly flung into the cinematic machinery. From 1914 to 1926 there had been steady progress, and in the films of 1922-1925 some remarkable things were being accomplished. Charlie Chaplin produced *The Pilgrim* in 1923, *The Gold Rush* in 1925 and *The Circus* in 1927. Robert Wiene's inventive and suggestive *The Cabinet of Dr. Caligari* was a film of 1919, James Cruze's *The Covered Wagon* of 1923; F. W. Murnau's *The Last Laugh* and Eisenstein's *The Battleship Potemkin* both were released in 1925. Out of these was developing a very pretty piece of critical theory, and it certainly looked as though the cinema, which for so long had dealt with impossible melodramatics and stupidly farcical situations, were coming to its own. A vast gulf yawned between the clumsy inanities of *The Fireman* and the subtleties of *The Gold Rush.* Directors and public alike were begining to sense potentialities they had hitherto never even conceived, and positive achievement seemed already to have been realised. Many in 1925 were prophesying great things for the years 1926 to 1930.

In reality, these years showed the cinema almost at its nadir. Sound came, and by one fell swoop most of the fondly established theories came crashing dismally to earth. It had been argued that the cinema was purely an art of visual appeal; that consequently everything should be subordinated to pictorial images; that sub-titles even were fundamentally unnecessary. In the earlier films continuity titles had been constant accompaniments of the displayed action, and by their means direct information and even portions of supposedly spoken speech were freely brought before the attention of the audience. That, argued the theorists, was wrong; the whole story ought to be developed by action and by suggestive symbols; these should stand unaided, and the art that used them seek no assistance, however slight, from the art of literature. The cinema, continued these theorists, is thus the most universal of all the arts. Literature is appreciated only by persons who are familiar with the particular language in which a book is written; painting has its limitations, for the basis of Western art is not that of the oriental; even music depends on a special training, so that the melodies of the Chinese strike strangely on our ears and Bach is incomprehensible in India. The cinema alone possesses the quality of complete universality. Based on fundamental things, it is the literature and the art of humanity. Before it opens out a vast, hitherto unimagined prospect, thrillingly enticing in its unexplored wonders.

Then sound: in a moment sound destroyed and shattered all this conceptioning. The cinema, according to the theorists, was cast back into hybrid mediocrity.

That something of this kind did actually occur, and that most certainly the promise of the years 1922-1925 was destroyed we must agree. We have to admit, too, that sound at first was very terrible. Those who attended performances of those first sound films will recall the alarming bass notes of the heroine and the hesitating uncertainty of the hero's tenor. You were never sure what was to come next and dwelt in constant dreadful expectancy. For some of us the new form had an exciting value of its own and we were prepared, knowing how much science had already accomplished, to credit a future refinement and measure of perfection. But to those whose dreams had been rudely broken by raucous voices, the sounds that came from the screen must have seemed ominous prognostications of doom and disaster. Even now many persons will not believe that the process of registering sounds on film-strips is the finest kind of recording hitherto achieved, or, admitting so much, stoutly deny the right of any words at all to interfere with the progress of the filmic story.

The third admission is this. Having discovered the sound film, or rather, having sound unwillingly thrust upon them, the producing companies, in a frantic agony of competitive desperation, immediately bethought them of the treasures of the stage. A play had action and words, they argued; the new sound film needed action and words; therefore it seemed reasonable to suppose that herein lay material ready for cinematic exploitation. Broadway and Shaftesbury Avenue were ransacked; from Paris and Berlin and Rome cables poured in to the offices announcing the success of this or that new drama; and scripts, eagerly sought for, rose in value. Authors and theatrical managers hastened to make hay in the shining of this cinematic sun; and the film, which had been developing its own technique, swept back to depend on the stage once more. All seemed lost.

In critical prose, the theorists put forward their many objections to the introduction of sound. They demonstrated to their own satisfaction that, the film being essentially an art of sight, the bringing in of sound rendered it impure. They emphasised the power of the cinema to control speed of movement and declared that with the coming of sound all this movement necessarily was slowed up. They had hailed the freedom of the cinema from the restrictions of the stage, and saw a return to full-face recording, with the movement of lips harmonised to the words that were spoken. They witnessed the rapid disappearance of the visual symbols so inherently cinematic.

Only after the passing of five or six years did the development of the cinema recover itself; indeed, the last two years are those which have brought us back to the conditions of 1925; but in bringing us back, they have also taken us forward and we are able to obtain a clearer view of filmic values than was possible in the earlier years of disruption.

MUSICAL ACCOMPANIMENT

In approaching this subject, it is to be realised that the film never has been without sound accompaniment. From the earliest "nickelodeon" days, music from a tinkling piano or a more formal orchestra has gone along with the display of the pictures on the screen. The reason is not far to seek. Normally, in life we associate sound and movement; on the stage sound hardly ceases unless for some particular purpose. Occasionally maybe the dramatist or director wishes to make comic capital out of a scene in which the characters remain silent; more commonly stage silence arouses a feeling of serious tension. It is the quietness before the breaking of a storm. To witness, without hearing a sound, a pure piece of miming, unless the miming be done in a wholly conventional manner, would become either tedious or over-straining; it is indeed observable that the vaudeville comedian whose skill lies in his actions nearly always demands an instrumental accompaniment from the orchestra. The film, in this, must bow to the same conventions as the stage. A restlessness would develop were we to witness only the actions, a restlessness dependent upon the potential alertness of our auditory nerves. We should expect sound and none would come. The musical accompaniment to silent films, therefore, simply occupied our attention and prevented the disappointment resultant upon a thwarted expectancy.

Often enough, this musical accompaniment assumed mimetic form. First of all, the music was clearly selected to accord with the situations. Delicate and melodious strains kept time with the lovers, and deep bass notes harmonised with the appearance of the heavy villain. From this the accompaniment proceeded to the actual suggestion at least of the sounds which would in reality have been heard in the given situations. Not all episodes lent themselves to this, but an organ would play a hymn tune in a church shot, wind instruments would play a march as the soldiers passed by, a sea symphony would come with the waves and rain music in a shot of deluge. Hence was but a step to the utilisation of special non-musical devices employed during the performances of some films—knocking at a door, rattling of pistol shots, pounding of horses' hooves.

So that, even before the introduction of the sound film, a definite approach had been made towards the introduction of mimetic sounds, in addition to the visual images. For some reason, these were felt by audiences and directors to be desirable. The sound-film, however, is fundamentally the talking-film, and with words enters in an intellectual content entirely different in character from either the musical accompaniment or the mimetic noises referred to above. It is this the theorists objected to. Before proceeding to examine these objections, it may be well to point out that the bringing in of incidental noises by means of synchronised recording can hardly itself be condemned. The recording method certainly is far superior to the sometimes erratic manufacturing of the noises by a member of the orchestra, and by its means the director may secure precisely the pitch and approximately the intensity he desires. The noises, it should be observed, need not be merely mimetic in the sense that they provide the sounds which would accompany real actions, nor need they come only when a particular visual image is cast on the screen. They often indeed may serve either for binding shot to shot or for emphasising the particular rhythm of the film. Thus in *The Informer,* after Gypo Nolan has given the particulars which will bring death to his friend, Frankie MacPhillip, we suddenly become aware of the insistent ticking of a clock on the wall. That shot ends, and in the interim between it and the next the ticking of the clock proceeds; proceeds, too, into the shot which shows Frankie at home with his mother and sister, where motivation is again provided by another wall-clock. Furthermore, this insistent ticking is caught up later by the tapping of a blind man's stick as Gypo slinks away from the Black-and-Tan headquarters. The noise possesses at once a subjective and an objective force: amply motivated in all three shots, its drumming persistency yet seems increased by individual awareness, now of time's passing, now of haunting retribution. Still further, a certain rhythmic beat is established thereby which gives some particular tone to the music with which this film is accompanied.

Sounds of this kind, however, as we have seen, may be kept distinct from words and introduced by those who theoretically would prohibit the use of dialogue. Charlie

Chaplin, for example, added to the silent mime a certain amount of sound effect in *City Lights,* but none of the sound had an intellectual significance. The "blah-blah-blah" of the civic orator was literally that and not built out of satirically conceived words. It is dialogue in formally conceived words, which still sticks in the throats of many.

In general, the objections to dialogue are based on a set of false assumptions, upon an unwillingness to consider the possible advantages to be derived from its use and from argumentation founded on observation of the worst in current film fare. Unquestionably, if dialogue were to mean that the fundamental cinematic methods were to be abandoned in favour of straight shooting, nothing could be said for it. To make the film merely a split-up version of a stage play were absurd; therein lies no future.

CONCENTRATION IN SOUND

The assumption that because a film and a stage play both use words therefore there is a likeness between them reveals its falsity just as soon as we stop to consider this question in detail. No doubt, many films of the present unimaginatively employ earlier technique and so fail to secure the greatest possible effectiveness within their command; even such a film as *The Scoundrel* by Hecht and MacArthur strangely erred in this respect, and, in spite of several interesting individual shots, proved unsatisfactory because its method was a combination of outworn cinematic devices and of devices associated with the stage. No use was made in it of symbolic imagery; nearly all the shots were straightforward ones, showing visually the lips of the speakers as they uttered their words; from close-up and medium shot we moved to close-up and medium shot in wearisome monotony; and the dialogue had not been toned down sufficiently for cinematic purposes.

The first thing we observe about cinematic dialogue is that, whereas in general a stage play demands constant talk, a film requires an absolute minimum of words. The essential basis of the cinema lies primarily in the realm of visual images, and such sound accompaniment as is admitted must be reduced to the barest necessaries. The distinction between the two forms becomes at once apparent if we pause to contrast some nineteenth century melodramas and some modern films in which there is excessive dialogue. The melodramas we shall condemn because their authors, in carelessness or haste, often allowed stage-direction, indicating action, to do the work which ought to have been accomplished by the use of words; while, on the other hand, we shall condemn a film which permits words to do what might have been achieved by means of moving forms on the screen. In essential principles drama and cinema stand distinct and separate; they are allied, no doubt, but allied in no wise other than as painting and sculpture, music and poetry, are allied. Lessing in his *Laocoon* demonstrated clearly that we ought to censure a sculptor for trying to do in marble what his fellow-artist so much more easily and effectively might do in words; and precisely the same holds true for cinema and drama.

Drama, certainly, is a concentrated form, and the author must guard against introducing any words or ideas which are not strictly germane to his theme and necessary for the building-up of his impression; but this concentration is increased a thousand-fold in the film. Part of the reason is that selectivity is more readily achieved in the latter, this selectivity being of certain kinds. First of all, we may take a typical scene in a play. That scene, let us say, introduces two men quarrelling. Now, so long as these men remain in the one location and are not interrupted by a third person, the quarrel scene has to be carried through in its entirety. Once start a conversation on the stage and it is difficult to bring it to a conclusion without developing the theme in some considerable fulness. The film, on the contrary, may arrest words or actions at any given moment, and this same scene might, in the hands of the cinematic director, reveal only the first movements and words, cutting all the intervening portions until the conclusion. The rest would be supplied by the imagination of the audience. At once we recognise why it is that a bare minimum of words is called for in the film and, concurrently, we appreciate the fact that in these snatches of conversation (because of the camera's ability to cut off the scene when required) greater point and neatness are demanded. An entirely diverse technique is summoned into play, for whereas the dramatic author will habitually aim at smoothness and continuity, with a dialogue moving steadily towards a good "curtain," the writer of a screen-play will strive towards the securing of variety, contrast and rapidly made points.

Further than this, however, does the power of concentration go. In ordinary life we normally see and hear only what we will ourselves to see or hear. Millions of objects appear before our eyes but of those millions only a small proportion actually is recorded in our minds, and of the corresponding millions of sounds few are consciously appreciated. Apart from this general fact we realise that sounds take on varying intensities in accordance with the subjective state of our own minds. As an example we may choose the ticking of a clock upon a wall. Usually the noise made by this clock will be completely ignored; although the sound, considered objectively, is constant and continually present, it simply ceases to exist so far as we are concerned. Occasionally for a brief moment the noise of its ticking will impinge itself on our senses, but generally, when this happens, we exercise our wills to dismiss it and again it ceases to exist. Imagine, however, an invalid, racked with fever, lying in the room; his mind is peculiarly sensitive so that to him the clock's ticking assumes an exaggerated importance. Try as he will, he cannot succeed in dismissing it from him and the more he strives to escape, the more insistent and terrifying the sounds become. Imagine, too, another person—a condemned prisoner awaiting the hour of his execution. For him the clock becomes a symbol of inexorable Time moving relentlessly on towards his final minute. The clock's ticking takes on for him also an exaggerated importance, only, instead of being irritating, it stands for a power of destiny he cannot control.

This single example may be sufficient to demonstrate that in real life we hear only certain of the myriad sounds around us and either deliberately select those of which we become conscious or else unconsciously dismiss the mass of those we remain unaware of. Sound is an objective thing, measurable by science; but the hearing of sound is subjective. On the stage, obviously there is considerable possibility of selection in this way—selection of dialogue and selection of "off-stage" noises both; but there can be little opportunity, save in a highly expressionistic play, of presenting either from the points of view of individual characters and consequently the possibility itself is limited. A ticking clock remains the same for all the persons introduced on the stage at one time, and, if we do wish to emphasise its importance for one character, we can do so in hardly any other way save by calling attention to the fact in actual speech.

For various reasons, therefore, dependent upon certain means peculiar to the cinema, filmic dialogue must, if it is to be truly characteristic and make full use of the opportunities offered to it, deviate considerably from dialogue characteristic of the stage. The selectivity is perhaps neither more nor less; it is simply different in kind and fully to appreciate this difference is the business of anyone connected, either creatively or critically, with the cinema.

SOUND CONTROL

The second essential difference between the use of sound (including speech) in the theatre and on the screen is that the former, in a variety of ways, bows absolutely to the will of the author and the director. Two kinds of sound there are which can be presented theatrically—the speech of the actors and "off-stage" noises. A little reflection, however, will show that both are extremely restricted in their range. The words spoken by the actors are restricted to the scope of utterance possessed by the performers themselves—for in this we cannot go beyond nature; and if for the "off-stage" noises any mechanical means is employed in the projection of the sounds clearly there is a fettering because of the danger of introducing too violent contrasts between the natural tones and those mechanically manufactured. In the cinema, on the other hand, all the sounds are mechanically reproduced and even although modern recording has achieved a fine sensitivity in rendering we can no more escape the consciousness that the sounds we hear are being presented to us through a medium than we can avoid the realisation that the forms thrown upon the screen are, not reality, but two-dimensional reproductions of reality. This means that the entire range of the sound effects in the film is immeasurably extended. In the process of projection the natural tones of the performers' voices may deliberately be made to acquire an increased flexibility and scope. Through the opportunities thus granted a singer's voice may be rendered into something which we could never hope to hear on the concert platform. Faulty notes can be deleted and a measure of perfection secured by a process of dovetailing all those portions which are flawless combined with that of cutting out those which introduce elements of a less satisfactory quality. Without creating any disturbance or confusion in the minds of the audience the power is granted to the director of developing and controlling a cinematic sound world even as he was granted the means of developing and controlling a cinematic time and a cinematic space.

Because of this extended range, allied to cognate qualities in the sound projection, the actual conversation which the players are to be given for utterance presents a series of problems new and distinct. By means of the purely cinematic tone much may be done acoustically towards the creation of mood and interest which, on the stage, would have to be accomplished through the use of intellectually conceived words. Furthermore, the fact that the words spoken by the actors and what would correspond to "off-stage" noises are harmonised by their both passing through the one medium permits of the introduction of effects securable but rarely and then with extreme difficulty in the theatre. It must, for example, be obvious to all that the suggestion on the stage of crowd noises generally fails in the impression which the dramatist or the director desires to produce. Whether a group of persons is trained to murmur and shout behind the scenes or a loud-speaker is employed, the device usually leaves much to be wished for. Just such effects form excellent cinematic material. Already we have seen how freely and impressively the camera may bring crowds within the range of its vision; masses of people whose presence in the theatre might seem forced and artificial may create powerful impression on the screen. In the same way the field of sound is so extended in the cinema that the acoustic qualities associated with these pictures may effectively be introduced there. Since all the sound heard comes to us through a mechanical medium, there can be no sense of discrepancy or conflict. Nor need this remain solely within the sphere covered by theatrical practice. *The Ghost goes West* introduced several shots which showed visually the Capitol at Washington and the Houses of Parliament in London, with accompanying sounds supposed to be the broadcasting of speeches on both sides of the Atlantic. Clearly this was a device which could reach realisation only in the cinema; for the theatre it would have been impossible.

Still more important is the fact that this mechanical reproduction, besides having the means of increasing the range of natural sound, provides opportunities for alteration and distortion. In the filmic version of *A Midsummer Night's Dream* one of the most effective scenes was that displaying the lovers' quarrel. A few rapid shots showed Hermia and Lysander, Helena and Demetrius in angry recrimination, and throughout the projection of these shots, without a break, we heard their voices in a confused babel of words. On the stage, of course, conversation among a group of characters may be made to overlap, but there could be no chance of proceeding so far as this in the building of an impression of voices excitedly distraught and confusedly intermingled. This example from *A Midsummer Night's Dream,* however, goes but one step beyond nature; no hint is provided there of the greater lengths to which the deliberate alteration of sound may go. One may state that there is no transformation of common tones and noises which is impossible in the cinema; for comic effect or for tragic we may do whatsoever we will with nature. Indeed, when we examine this subject, we realise that precisely the same means of manipulation exist in the realm of sound as exist in the realm of visual images. Slow motion and accelerated motion can be applied to sounds and to the objects of sight as we may desire. We may use the device of double exposure and lay one series of sounds or noises upon another. We may even project words in reverse just as we may show characters on the screen proceeding in backward motion. The fade-in, the fade-out and the dissolve—all of these have their acoustic counterparts; by their means it is easy to have one set of sounds intermingle with another set, to create just such a juxtaposition as we have seen possible in the field of visual images.

How far this control removes the writing of a screenplay from the writing of a stage-drama must be immediately manifest. Acoustic montage has to be applied here in the same way as visual montage is applied to the images fixed on the frames. We are dealing here, not with a selection of sounds from nature, but with a collection of sounds recorded on strips of film, each in its own way distinct from the original which gave it birth, all to be wrought into a harmony by the skill of the author and director.

SOUND SUBJECTIVITY

On the power which the film possesses of abstracting from objective reality particular sounds heard by individual characters and on its power to transform these sounds at will clearly depends the film's ability to suggest, by oral means, psychological processes at which the stage can but hint. With sounds as with visual images, there is the same ease in moving from an objective to a subjective approach. Without the slightest difficulty, a shot, or a series of shots, may be introduced giving the sounds heard by one selected character and not by others introduced in the plot. We might have, for instance, a medium shot showing four persons with no accompaniment save the dialogue given to them, and then a close shot showing one of these persons accompanied by such sounds (external noises in addition to chosen words) as that particular individual is hearing at the moment.

Before going further, it is well to emphasise here that, while dramatic dialogue must always be directly presented, filmic dialogue may be introduced in a variety of ways, of which by far the least interesting is that which shows persons speaking. Absolute synchronisation of lip-movement and of words uttered may be desirable and necessary, but we do not always need, in fact we rarely need, to see the lips at work while the sounds impinge themselves on our ears. In the realm of visual movement, as we have seen, there is the possibility in the cinema of presenting merely part of an object; the pawnbroker's hands therein stand for the whole figure of the man who, in a dramatic treatment of the Dickensian theme, would have had to be brought physically on the stage. Precisely similar opportunities are offered in the realm of sound, for the film may freely provide the words of persons whom we do not see, not because these persons are concealed behind screens or curtains, but because we choose to focus our attention elsewhere. Even in that small passage from *The Barretts of Wimpole Street* there is demonstrated a typical utilisation of this device. Flush is let into the hall; from an inner room comes a voice, the voice of Barrett, and, hearing it, the dog drops his tail and slinks upstairs. While we are looking at Flush, we hear Barrett. No doubt this particular effect, save for the acting of the dog, might be reproduced on the stage; but from this we proceed further. By means of groupings and of positions, a theatrical director may suggest what particularly he wants his audience to observe, but never may we be positively assured that the indications will be appreciated or carried out in realisation. Within the cinematic sphere, the director is sole judge of what the audience shall see and hear; because of the means at his command he can rest assured that every single thing he chooses will be brought fully to the attention of the spectators and that there will be no chance of having certain dearly cherished and carefully planned effects lost or disregarded through the straying of attention elsewhere. From his point of view, therefore, dialogue assumes functions and must be made to serve purposes entirely different from those associated with theatrical conversation.

Here another aspect of the subject calls for consideration. On the stage (unless in some bizarre and highly experimental productions) the dialogue heard by the audience is associated directly with the characters set at the moment within the proscenium frame. This, as has been demonstrated, need not hold for the cinema where sound heard and objects seen may be, if desired, wholly separated. The result is that the filmic author and director are granted certain opportunities denied to the dramatist and the theatrical director. Sound and visual images may agree in synchronisation, indeed, it is possible to agree that commonly this combination will form the staple basis of any ordinary film. On the other hand, infinite variety is achievable in different directions. An impression of strong contrast may be evoked by showing, say, a picture of a man in despair while a jazz melody insistently throbs in our ears. Another impression may be summoned forth by making the two (the visual and the acoustic) agree without synchronisation in mood and spirit. The scene of grief might, for example, be given increased tension and poignancy by having the picture accompanied, not by words, but by the whimpering or moaning as of some animal in pain. Or else, perhaps, the words are left and the visual images changed, as in a scene where we hear the voices of two lovers murmuring their endearments while on the screen we watch the slow ripple of waves upon the sand or the gentle tossing of boughs in a forest. Further opportunities may be exemplified by a series of shots in *Strike Me Pink* where during the singing of a song suggestive of violent emotion the visual images were presented in a series of exceedingly short, sharply delineated and abruptly divided pictures. The possibilities of securing variety by such means are indeed unmeasured. All we need to do in order to appreciate this is to think of some simple situation —let us say, a miser bent over his treasured gold—and imagine the diverse ways in which the film might treat it.

We might have the miser soliloquising, with lip movements synchronised, or silent himself with a whispering voice suggesting his inner thoughts, or silent again with the groaning of some hungry wretch coming to us from outside his window, or silent still with the accompaniment of immaterialised and fantastic sounds expressive in some way of his greed; or else we might completely change the approach, allowing the jingling clink of the coins as he counts them to become accompaniments to pictures which do not introduce the figure of the miser at all—pictures calculated, by their imagic agreement or by their contrast, to bring forth more strongly the impression desired.

In order to make this absolutely clear it is possibly best to retrace our steps a moment and take a perfectly simple example of filmic non-agreement in acoustic and visual terms. Such an example is provided in that scene of *The Barretts of Wimpole Street* when Barrett enters Elizabeth's room in the midst of Henrietta's hilarious polka:

BEDROOM FULL SHOT—

Henrietta has stopped dead in the centre of the room. The others stand rooted to their places. The silence is deadly.

CUT TO:

CLOSE SHOT FLUSH

He descends quietly from the foot of Elizabeth's couch and pads discreetly—CAMERA PANNING WITH HIM—over to his basket. He clambers in, and lies down, his back to the camera.

CUT TO:

ELIZABETH'S ROOM—CLOSE SHOT BARRETT

He stands motionless just beyond the threshold looking before him with a perfectly expressionless face.

Voice of Elizabeth

Good evening, Papa.

The camera then proceeds to pick up Barrett again and we see him speaking: but a moment later the same device is repeated:

CLOSE SHOT HENRIETTA & OCTAVIUS

Henrietta

I—I beg your pardon, Papa.

Voice of Barrett

And may I ask what you were doing as I came into the room?

Henrietta

I was showing Ba how to polk.

CUT TO:

CLOSE UP BARRETT

He looks incredulous disgust.

Barrett

To . . . polk?

Voice of Henrietta

How to dance the polka.

Barrett

I see.

An analysis of this sequence indicates the rapid shifting of attention. First, it is concentrated upon Henrietta, arrested suddenly in her dance (visual only); then it moves to Flush, symbolic of the spirit of the human actors, cowed by Barrett's presence (visual, for symbolic effect); is fixed upon Barrett, with Elizabeth's voice coming through (visual and indirect sound); turns back to Henrietta, with the voice of Barrett heard (visual and both direct and indirect sound); and finally concentrates on Barrett with Henrietta's faltering accents indicating her fear (visual and both direct and indirect sound). Variety is provided here and an emphasis, possibly not greater than might have been secured on the stage, but assuredly divergent in essential principle from that.

The use of the unseen voice has many applications in the filmic telling of a story. Only occasionally on the stage, by the use of non-directional recording apparatus or by that of the aside, can an approach be made towards the creation of words apart from those spoken in conversation by the actors seen by the audience. God's voice may thus descend from the clouds to a devout Noah, O'Neill may employ the aside in *Strange Interlude* to suggest inner thought, unexpressed externally in life, and Shakespeare may have his heroes unburden their hearts in words through the medium of soliloquy. Such methods, however, seem only too often forced and strained, while of means to project the unarticulated voices of madness and hallucination there are none. All this may readily be accomplished in the cinema. In the same way that *The Informer* showed momentarily a subjective mental image in Gypo Nolan's mind while his eyes rested on the model of the liner, so momentarily are presented the voices which well up within his own consciousness and to him appear audible as those actually spoken by his companions. When his conscience recreates the image of the murdered Frankie, Frankie's voice takes shape and warns him that he is lost, that without the aid of his friend's brains he can do naught. Similarly, too, in *The Scoundrel* words, which may be those of fate or merely the hallucinations of a dying man, sound while we look upon the floating body in the whirling waste of waves. The mother in *So Red The Rose* hears her son calling, and, as we ride with her when she sets out to find his body, the mental voice comes whisperingly through to us. Immense possibilities are here, both in the creation of themes specifically designed for the film and in the re-treatment of themes already known to the stage. A film of *Hamlet* thus might articulate much more of the hero's imaginings than the stage soliloquies allowed, and Joan of Arc's supposedly heaven-sent admonitions could take actual filmic form before an audience. By the employment of a whispered intensity, these words could never be mistaken for the words of living persons consciously uttering their thoughts; spectators, however untutored, would find no difficulty in appreciating their force and significance.

LINKAGE BY SOUND

Already something has been said concerning the linking of shots in the cinema, but this subject, introducing a fresh use of sound, deserves a trifle more attention. In a theatrical performance, as we have seen, the divisions in the action are relatively few and not many opportunities are offered to the director for the binding together of part and part. Occasionally an attempt is made in this way; recent examples were provided by Georg Bruckner's *Elizabeth and Essex* and the same author's *Races,* when words spoken in one scene were caught up in the scene immediately following or running concurrently. The device, however, is not essentially dramatic and even when skilfully handled, generally lacks conviction. At the most it may be employed in one single section of a play. We found the movement of the savage tribal chant into the hymn-singing of Munro's *Progress* exceedingly effective, but the employment of a similar concatenation in other scenes would have been deemed monotonous or ridiculous.

In a film, on the other hand, the shots are so numerous and the intermission periods so brief that linking of one set of images to another becomes generally desirable and certainly easy of attainment. That linkage usually is secured by visual means, but sound presents the opportunity of diversifying the method of binding the shots and of producing slightly different emotional results. A simple example of such sound linkage appears in the Micawber scenes of *David Copperfield,* where the wailing of the child joins shot and shot together; that child is shown in one picture, as we wait for the next shot its wailing cry is still heard, and while we watch the second shot, although the child itself is not in the picture, the cry persists. The ticking of the clock in *The Informer* illustrates a further use of this device, three distinct scenes being connected by its means. Difficult indeed would it be exactly to analyse our aesthetic and emotional reactions during the hearing of this sound. In one respect, the realistic motivation is complete—that is to say, in the latter example there is no reason why we should not hear the ticking of the second clock. On the other hand, we realise two things: first, that the ticking is exaggeratedly loud and, second, that it has harmonised with or forms a continuation of the sound given forth by the other. With the latter we shared empathically in Gypo's nervous expectation, and with the former, although Gypo is not present, indeed has remained far off in the Black and Tan headquarters, we watch the action at least partly through his imagination. The movements of the characters are objective, certainly, but at the same time we know that these movements are precisely those which Gypo was conjuring up in his brain while he dwelt on the effect of the information he had given. The linkage here is thus not entirely objective; we are carried forward from shot to shot emotionally.

Further possibilities in treatment of cinematic dialogue and in linkage effects were revealed in a short sequence of an otherwise not too imaginative film, *The Man Who Broke the Bank at Monte Carlo*.

In that sequence we are taken to Interlaken where the hero, Ronald Colman, has made the acquaintance of the heroine, Joan Bennett. The business of the director is to show the progress of their friendship. On the stage all that could have been accomplished would have been the presentation of a single scene in which Colman testified to his adoration. Normally in cinematic treatment there would have been a series of scenes each with a short passage of conversation between the pair; but in this particular story it was obviously expedient to keep the girl as silent as possible while, on the other hand, the particular terms Colman found to testify to his love did not really matter. All we were concerned with was the fact that he had fallen madly in love with her and told her so. The entire story, therefore, was narrated in three closely associated shots. In the first the two were riding, in the second they were boating and in the third they stood after dinner upon the terrace of the hotel. These unrelated pictorial shots were bound by words; during the first we heard Colman utter six words, the beginning of a sentence, during the second he was carrying on that sentence, and during the third the sentence was completed. Nothing could have been better devised to suggest the constant reiteration of his passion, while the association of the pictures with the words clearly indicated the various occasions he took to reveal his state of mind. Visually, orally and by combined linkage effect the impression was effectively and arrestingly given.

Closely connected with this question goes the question of sub-titles. Sub-titles, we might have imagined, would have naturally vanished with the disappearance of the silent film, but we can still see them in at least a few of the current products. In general, they are to be condemned, although very occasionally they may serve a special purpose of their own. The test, probably, ought to be whether they can be dispensed with or their information supplied by more normal cinematic methods. Judged according to this standard, their use in three or four recent films was faulty. *The Informer* started with a perfectly needless reference to Judas casting down the thirty pieces of silver. The quotation printed on the screen did nothing to add either to the story or to the appreciation of Gypo's character; rather did it serve to distract because it raised an assumption that something was to be developed in the theme which was never carried out and never even projected. *Les Miserables,* similarly, started with a few words of information which aided not a whit towards the understanding of the plot. Perhaps preliminary notes of this kind are not wholly to be deplored, but, if introduced, they had better come as frank directional information along with the name of the actors, reproducing thus what might have gone in a theatre program note. It seems a mistake to put them in Gothic or other "harmonising" letters and to throw them on the screen as the first shot of the film itself.

Much more dangerous are the titles within a film. One of

this kind suddenly intruded itself in the course of *David Copperfield,* where a caption drew our attention to the fact that, having pursued the fortunes of the young David, we were now to follow his career in manhood. Even more disturbing were those in *Peter Ibbetson.* Among them was a sentence telling us that Peter was confined in a prison, set amid bleak northern moors. To have displayed these moors before us, to have suggested the dank and the dreary wastes, would have been a simple cinematic task; the sub-title was manifestly a wrong procedure. Another similar employment of the printed words appeared in *The Little Minister.* There one shot shows Babby scribbling her note in the minister's Bible; the next action shot reveals the minister himself finding this note on opening the Bible while he stands in the pulpit. Between the one and the other a number of days is supposed to elapse, and, to indicate this, a notice "On the following Sunday . . ." was inserted. Once more we cannot escape feeling that the lapse of time could have been indicated by means, either visual or oral, more in accord with the cinematic style. Final examples may be taken from *A Tale of Two Cities.* Here there was a foreword title, giving a fairly long quotation stating that this "was the best of times" and "the worst of times . . . in short, it was a period very like the present." Into this foreword title faded a scene on Shooter's Hill, the Dover Road, with, superimposed upon it, a caption reading "England—The Dover Road, A Certain Evening Late in the 18th Century." Later on we were shown an obviously French roadway with characteristic rows of poplars and once more came the superimposed caption, "France." Hardly any better examples could be found than these. Maybe a "program note" might have been admitted, but the initial quotation was of doubtful value, while the information about the Dover road and the French roadway was either otiose or a confession of weakness. For the whole series of titles there was no excuse. Nor was there excuse for the title which accompanied an aristocratic banquet scene:—"This was the Warning," with its long-winded terms. When the revolution starts and messengers are sent galloping over the land, the visual pictures were amply sufficient to emphasise the action, and consequently another superimposed title was worse than valueless:—"Over the Countryside the Message of Hate went forth: Death to the Aristos! Death to the Innocent as well as the Guilty! Death to all Aristos! Death to their Friends! Death to their Servants! Smite them all, the Root and the Branch! Death!" Equally false was the commentary, "And from the Slum of St. Antoine came the Answer: 'Down with the Bastille'," while this plethora of printed signs reached its most absurd expression in a series of questions:— "Why?" "WHY?" "WHY?" we read in increasing size of letters and in increasing wonderment. Even a well prepared scenario like *Anna Karenina* superimposed a useless "Moscow" over a picture which, because it concentrated on "the characteristic domes of the Kremlin," clearly told its own story.

That the creator of a screen-play and a director are here presented with a serious difficulty is, of course, not to be denied, but we may at the same time assert that the solving of the problem ought to be attempted cinematically and not in the way of literary narrative. Filmically both the passage of time and the establishing of setting had better be indicated either by means of visual symbols or, if absolutely necessary, by means of spoken words. The former method is generally the more satisfactory; but in the sound film words, too, may be used for this purpose as they are used in a stage play, although, with the much greater concentration demanded by the cinema, rarely is there the opportunity granted for leisurely time exposition. Each word has to do so much more in a film than in a play that but sparing use can be made of oral indications of this kind.

Normally, we may agree that, in spite of the difficulties, mere falling back on informative captions is an unimaginative escape; ample justification is there for saying that, by symbolic images—visual or verbal—a way should be found for bringing the lapse of time or the locality directly before the public. Occasionally a device of the kind employed in *So Red the Rose* may be employed—the providing of information by some titles disguised as filmic material, in this instance through what purported to be Civil War bulletins chalked on a board; but such a device, although wrought into the general plan, clearly is not to be used with any frequency. However transformed, it remains a printed caption, and to that almost anything is preferable. Even the use of an unseen announcer's voice, the Voice of Time, would have been better than the introduction of the printed words in *David Copperfield*. Strangely enough, this device, although known on the stage from an early period, seems not to have been much exploited in the film. There would appear to be no valid reason why it should not meet a need, although, as with all things in cinematic art, experience from actual trial alone could provide a definite answer.

Having thus surveyed some of the basic principles involved in the sound film, we may turn to a brief consideration of the film scenario or screen-play in its entirety. Already have been demonstrated the essential facts that cinematic dialogue must be much more economic in its effects than dialogue in a play, that we expect in it not the complete development of a conversation from beginning to end but a series of suggestions concerning that conversation's course, that the subjective frequently must be called into service alongside the objective, and that the words introduced often must play a double part, directly presenting a scene and indirectly linking that scene to the one immediately following. Dependent on these principles is another, that, in order to secure economy, visual images are preferable to words if these visual images are sufficient to convey the impression desired. Fundamental to the cinema is that which is presented to the eye; this must ever take chief place. Words spoken occupy a secondary position; and printed words may only occasionally be called into service. *A Tale of Two Cities* presented one sequence which illustrates this clearly. Mme. Defarge has just told La Vengeance that the man who had kept Dr. Manette in prison for eighteen years was the Marquis St. Evremonde and has added that, for other reasons as well, this nobleman occupies "a place of honour" on her "register." This information could hardly have been presented visually; therefore the dialogue is right and just. Right and just, too, are the following wholly visual shots:—

CAMERA PANS DOWN the shawl that she is knitting, until we come to almost the top of the shawl. The knitting is covered with simplified designs of the crests of armorial bearings of the aristocratic families. The first is the same as the crest of the carriage door of the Marquis St. Evremonde. From the crest on her register,

DISSOLVE TO:

THE SAME CREST
On a carriage door of a coach, which is moving quickly. PULL CAMERA BACK and reveal the Marquis, sitting nonchalantly and casually—speaking to an attendant, Moreau.

After a series of shots introducing words and actions (the coach brought to a stop when it runs over the little child of Gaspard and setting off again) there is a further dissolve into a picture of

CHATEAU EVREMONDE
The Marquis' carriage comes over moat, and comes to stop at porte-cochere. He alights amid lackeys—turns, goes off stage.

This, again, is followed by:—

THE CHATEAU EVREMONDE. CLOSE SHOT THE COAT OF ARMS OVER THE MAIN DOOR.

There can be no doubt but that by such visual means the implications of the story and the relationship of the characters are fully and effectively portrayed. On the other hand we may reasonably criticise adversely the latter part of *The Informer,* a film otherwise well planned, because of its failure to permit the visual precedence over the oral. The story of this film was largely told in visual pictures up to the last court-martial scene, and that scene somehow proved less satisfying than the earlier shots. The reason well may lie in the fact that words there were substituted for movements. Movement there was, of course, but not sufficient attention had been paid to the necessity of securing an absolute economy in the speeches and of allowing the eyes to serve as instruments for the imagination. How fully possible this is was shown in *Chapayev,* where the character and achievements of the hero were delineated visually in such a manner that a spectator who knew no Russian could, even without the aid of sub-titles, follow at least the main outlines of the plot and appreciate Chapayev's virtues and vices as conceived by the director.

It is but natural that, since the film started with silent images cast on a screen, greater proficiency should in general be displayed in the controlling and determining of visual sequences than in welding words into suitable cinematic form. Of this, too, a good example is provided in *A Tale of Two Cities.* Whereas the shots showing the capture of the Bastille were brilliantly managed (in the screen-play conception, if not in actual direction), with judicious variety both in the incidents delineated and in the camera angles, the conversational portions of the film were weak. Soliloquy was permitted to intrude when Carton meditated on the distinction between himself and Darnay; and soliloquy must be judged a thing essentially belonging to the stage, a convention determined by the theatre's restrictions in the possibility of displaying inner thought. In many parts, too, the words came in long monotonous sequences, lacking diversity. In the screen-play, throughout two entire pages Carton and Darnay converse without any attempts being made to co-ordinate movement in the pictures presented and movement in the words. The storming of the Bastille, on the other hand, exhibited careful planning and genuine appreciation of cinematic values. Bare feet clattering over cobblestones, independent shots showing selected citizens leaving their shops to join the crowd, the mob marching, that mob joined by others, the mob seen from the castle walls, the drawbridge rising and bearing with it a young man who is eventually forced to fall, rapid short shots of individual members of the mob and of the troops, the firing of the cannon, the arrival of the French soldiers, and the final fall of the fortress. The way in which this was handled, particularly the skill used in quickening the tempo and reducing the length of the shots in accordance with the increase in tension and excitement, left little to be desired. The contrast between the methods employed here and those employed in the treatment of dialogue is thoroughly characteristic.

While emphasising the importance of the visual images, we must at the same time note that sound is not a mere appendage in the film. The introduction of words has brought into being a new form, these words and their power frequently determining the shape which a film play will take. Perhaps, in order to emphasise this a few concrete examples may be taken, and first it will be convenient to start with one where it is possible to compare closely stage and cinematic versions of the same theme. Of all modern plays perhaps *The Barretts of Wimpole Street* is among the best-known, and consequently it will not be unfitting to select that and the accompanying screen-play for examination. In the play's second act, as will be recalled, several themes were developed—principally those of Henrietta's love of Surtees Cook and of Elizabeth's first meeting with Robert Browning. The whole of the action during this series of scenes—indeed during the entire length of the stage-play—was set in Elizabeth's room.

A comparison of this with the corresponding episodes in the film becomes highly instructive. First of all, there is, of course, no act division. Following the play, the film makes Elizabeth ask Wilson to draw the curtains and extinguish the lamp, but the movement that follows introduces several essentially cinematic features. The camera proceeds from a general shot of the room to a close-up of Elizabeth, and thence "pans" over to a close-shot of the window. During the second of these we see "one of the faded flowers in the vase" shed "its petals on the table."

Deliberately this shot is made to dissolve in order to provide continuity of impression: the scene just shown drifts into another of the same window framing a winter view. The camera now draws nearer, tilts downwards and presents us with a glimpse of the street below where we see Henrietta emerging with a surreptitious air from the doorway. Here comes the first major departure from the stage action. Besier obviously was forced to employ a trick in order to get Surtees Cook within Elizabeth's room, and, equally obviously he was denied the opportunity of showing anything of the clandestine meetings between Cook and Henrietta. The ubiquitous camera, however, can tilt itself downwards and, having caught Henrietta outside, may follow her until she meets her lover at the nearby pillar-box. The few phrases of the stage Henrietta's reported conversation are legitimately expanded here into a section of dialogue which serves to indicate the relations between this pair and the force which separates them.

The next shot in the film shows Elizabeth on her couch, reading a book before an open fire. Wilson moves in to clear away the dishes, and there ensues the substance of the play's dialogue concerning the unfinished lunch and the incomprehensibilities of *Sordello*. This is presented by means of the general shot referred to, a close shot of Wilson as she stops in surprise, a medium shot of Elizabeth and Wilson while the former reads the passage from Browning's poem. Immediately upon the close of this action (without any break) Arabel and Bella enter, Bella then announcing her engagement. At this there is a cut to a close shot of the door, through which Henrietta comes dazedly. Through several shots the conversation proceeds until Bella leaves, confident of her power to win Barrett's consent for the appearance of Henrietta at her marriage. Left alone with Elizabeth, Henrietta tells that Surtees Cook has asked her to marry him and that "of course she accepted him—and said that she couldn't." This is interrupted by the arrival of a note from Browning, announcing that he is downstairs and waiting to see Elizabeth. Here the screen version, by presenting a reading of the note and some accompanying comments, adds a trifle to the dialogue of the play. After some hesitation Browning is admitted. First we see Elizabeth nervously waiting; Henrietta's voice is heard; Browning enters and greets her. With some considerable movement of the camera, this scene continues up to the beginning of the discussion concerning his poetry. Then we get a close-up of Flush, "sitting up in his basket, gazing interestedly at the visitor." This shot is caught up by Browning's turning to the dog and addressing some of his remarks to it. Through a series of varied shots the scene proceeds, while Elizabeth confronts him with the obscurities of *Sordello*. That finished, a long—probably too long—shot follows in which Browning testifies to his adoration. Then the talk ceases: Elizabeth rises shakily and manages to reach the window, her movement being momentarily broken by a short glimpse of Flush as "he watches his mistress with grave eyes." From above we see the street as Elizabeth sees it and watch the figure of Browning marching bravely down it.

Thus ends the second main section of the film, corresponding to the play's second act. Clearly the action follows that of the drama fairly closely, but precisely because of this close approximation we may discern more easily the differences between the dramatic and the cinematic methods. Flush plays no part in this act on the stage; unless with a specially trained dog his performance therein would have been entirely impossible. In the film, on the other hand, he can be made to play an important rôle and symbolically to arouse the audience's imagination. A mere comic element in the drama, he becomes almost a protagonist in the film, for it is he who both begins and closes the entire action. The exploitation of his rôle is perfectly justifiable. Justifiable, too, is the symbolic treatment of the falling petals. The effect would have been insecurable on the stage both because of physical difficulties presented in producing such a trick and because the distance of the spectators would rob the device of any real significance. It is just such a device as the cinema legitimately may use. Still more important is the use made of a combined objective and subjective approach towards certain things—concentration on what she sees and concentration on the picture of Elizabeth herself.

All of these, however, lie within the sphere of visual images, and at the moment we are concerned mainly with sound. Much of the play's conversation in this section of the film has been curtailed, and rightly so in view of the different conditions in presentation; but one episode has been added, the direct displayal of Henrietta's love affair. Without a doubt, we feel that the insertion of this episode was right, and, believing so, at once we recognise that, just as the theatre has certain *scènes à faire* without seeing which an audience is dissatisfied, in the cinematic narrative other *scènes à faire* are demanded, including material which in a play we should be content to have described for us. Following along this line of thought, we may well ask ourselves the question whether indeed more deviation still was not demanded in this cinematic treatment of *The Barretts of Wimpole Street.* In particular one might argue that in the cinema more preparation is demanded for Browning's entrance than is provided by the sudden sending-in of the letter; one might express the belief that several shots showing Browning in his own surroundings would have been desirable, thus by presenting contemporaneous events in his apartment and in Elizabeth's sitting-room bringing that tension which is peculiarly securable by these cinematic means. Indeed, there is a need for just such a scene here as is given later in the screen-play when, after watching Elizabeth write her letter to Browning, we find the scene fading into the poet's study, and there listen to Wilson's words, first to the housekeeper and later to Browning himself. The presence in this study of books by and articles on Elizabeth is used to emphasise the passionate devotion he accords her. In the play we know it is impossible to see Browning at the moment he receives her note; realising that no difficulty is presented in the cinematic treatment, this is a scene we positively demand. There can be no doubt but that this is not only thoroughly in harmony with the cinematic technique but also a very effective way of telling Browning's story; and we recognise that something of this kind was required also before the poet's appearance in Elizabeth's room.

Already examples have been given of the way in which concurrent events of this kind may be effectively introduced by means of visual images alone; an indication of the manner in which they may be used to build up a filmic narrative by combined employment of sound and image is provided by the beginning of *Private Lives.* This film, after a general shot of a marriage ceremony, opens with a composition shot of a church interior taken over the back of the minister:

Bride and bridegroom stand side by side at the chancel rail. Sybil looks up at Elyot with a demurely happy smile to which he responds with some restraint. The hymn ends. The parson, book in hand, takes a step towards the bridal pair.

The Parson

Dearly beloved brethren, we are gathered together here, in the sight of God and . . .
As he speaks, DISSOLVE INTO INT(ERIOR) FRENCH *MAIRIE*—COMP(OSITION) SHOT—DAY (Shooting from back of *Maire*). The voice of the English Parson dissolves into that of the little *Maire,* bearded, beribboned and important, who is gabbling the concluding half of the Civil marriage service in fluent French. Victor, the bridegroom, seems a little dubious as to the propriety of this French ceremony; Amanda is quite at ease, not to say amused.

There follows here a comic interlude, during which the *Maire* continues reciting his service. At the end of this

He returns—ignoring the laughter of the villagers—to the bridal pair CAMERA PANNING WITH HIM and continues his rapid gabbling of the service as we DISSOLVE INTO EXT(ERIOR) SKY—LONG SHOT—DAY

From the heart of a great white cloud comes the sound of a plane in flight and in a moment the plane itself emerges from the clouds and flies toward camera.

DISSOLVE INTO

INT(ERIOR) PLANE—CLOSE SHOT—SYBIL AND ELYOT.

This shot, concentrating on the young couple as they sit in the plane, introduces some dialogue which indicates that Sybil is Elyot's second bride. It in turn dissolves into

EXT(ERIOR) FERRY—MEDIUM SHOT

Victor's roadster is being towed across a river on an old fashioned ferry worked by a sturdy peasant from the bank. The monotonous squeak proceeds from the winch the man is turning.

CAMERA MOVES TO A CLOSE SHOT of Victor and Amanda. Victor holds on his lap a neat and shining little lunch basket. Amanda leans against Victor's shoulder interestedly examining the contents. Victor looks down at her tenderly.

Some dialogue again follows and during it we learn that Amanda has been previously married to Elyot. At once the significance and relationship of the two sets of shots become apparent; and when we turn from these to first the exterior and then the interior of a Riviera hotel the purpose of both comes with tense expectancy to us. Anxiously we watch Elyot and Sybil alight from their taxi and get supplied with a terrace suite, followed by Victor and Amanda who likewise are accommodated with a terrace suite on the same floor.

The gradual drawing together of two apparently unrelated episodes, with only occasional and vague clues, provided partly by visual images, partly by words, seems one of the specific functions of cinematic narrative. This method may, of course, be used both for comic and for serious effect: it may be employed to arouse laughter, or romantic expectancy, or the terror of an almost tragic emotion. On the rhythm of the shots and the temper introduced into them will depend the effect they have on us. From this consideration must spring a realisation of what an opportunity was lost in *The Barretts of Wimpole Street.* Cinematically, the story offered a good chance for such double action in the Elizabeth Barrett-Robert Browning relationship; nay further, for the adequate unfolding of the story more was required than the sudden receipt by the former of the latter's note. Maybe there was a justification here for keeping as closely as possible to the theme development of the play in that this play was so well known that serious deviations might have met with a considerable amount of adverse comment. So far the method employed may be defended; but considering this film as a film, and therefore as something entirely distinct from any stage production, we might well demand freer handling and greater use of that which the cinema may give which the stage cannot.

An examination of other films leads to similar judgments. Let us take a simple example, *Bonnie Scotland,* in which the irrepressible Laurel and Hardy were featured. In that we started with a street in a small Scots town; the pair go to an hotel, stating that they have come to claim a legacy; they proceed to the solicitor's office where, to show their identity, they display jail cards and explain they have crossed the Atlantic in a cattle-boat. No doubt, by these sequences a few elements of surprise are secured, but one may well ask the question whether, in view of the fact that we have here a series of scenes taking place in what is fundamentally one locality (the Scots town), the method employed is not closer to the dramatic than to the cinematic. The journey on the cattle-boat and the jail experiences are indicated mainly by a kind of retrospective narrative; and retrospective narrative is alien to the general methods of the film. One may suggest that much more comic effect might have been attained by opening the film in a Mid-Western prison, with following scenes of escape, pursuit, safe stowage in a cattle-boat and arrival in the Scots town. By this means the story would have been told in more effectively cinematic terms.

Another example, taken from a serious film, *A Tale of Two Cities,* corroborates this judgment. Undoubtedly the freedom of the film brings it nearer in structure to the novel than the drama, where a conventional limitation and restriction is demonstrably essential; but simply to follow the plan of a novel in the preparing of a screen-play is a procedure as erroneous as the faithful reproduction on the screen of dramatic form. This, unfortunately, is the scheme of *A Tale of Two Cities.* Starting with a quotation, we take up the contents of Dickens's first chapter, see the Dover Mail lumbering up Shooter's Hill and hear the mysterious message, "Recalled to Life." Next we come to the Royal George Hotel, Dover, where Lorry tells Lucie Manette of her father's imprisonment and rescue. Straightaway, we move over to Paris and have presented before us the tabloided contents of Dickens' chapter in which he describes so magnificently the broken barrel and the trickling blood-red wine spreading along the narrow street. Next we are introduced to Defarge's wine-shop whither Lucie comes to reclaim her father. No doubt the sequence of incidents does not lack interest, but the arrangement seems much better adapted for the purposes of prose narrative than for those of the cinema. The information regarding Dr. Manette's imprisonment must perforce be presented retrospectively as must several other matters relating to the principal *dramatis personæ*. A much more effective arrangement might easily have been found than this simple one of following the novel's structure, and no doubt increased interest might have arisen from a carrying of the action back beyond the point from which it is made to start. Long passages of informative dialogue such as that between Lucie Manette and Lorry appear generally unfitted for treatment in the film.

Quite apart from narrative values, too, the presence of sound must in the future play a determining part in the creation of the screen-play. One example, and that a simple one, may serve. On the stage an effect may be produced of stillness moving into swift action or of quietness giving way to loud sound. Such effects, however, will be conditioned by the physical limitations of the stage and by the sets necessarily employed. By filmic methods something more and of a different kind may be secured. At the beginning of *Top Hat,* for example, the first shot shows a wall-plate informing us that the building we are about to enter is The Thackeray Club, London; a second shot displays a notice saying that silence must be observed by members in the club rooms, the way being thus prepared for a shot of a lounge in which a dozen men are seated, each solemnly buried behind a copy of *The Times*. Among them, clearly anxious impishly to create a disturbance, sits Fred Astaire. The silence and decorum are intensified further by the angry glances and expressions of offended dignity when a waiter inadvertently clinks one wine-glass against another and when Astaire himself makes his newspaper rustle in the process of unfolding it. The path is cleared for a strong contrast. The immediately obvious contrast comes when Astaire, leaving the lounge, stands at the doorway and startles the members by executing a few staccato dance steps; but a much more important contrast follows when at length, in his own apartment, his nimble feet start to beat out their amazing rhythms. The ease with which a film can move from set to set offers innumerable opportunities for sound contrasts of this larger kind and manifestly these opportunities must condition to a certain extent the composition of the preliminary screen-play.

That, within the past two or three years, vast advances have been made in technical knowledge and in artistic sensibility to cinematic requirements needs no demonstration; but obviously complete mastery has not yet been attained. For the securing of that mastery is required not only a great amount of experimentation but also an exhaustive examination of cinematic devices and of cinematic principles, such as the stage has had in its possession for centuries. Critical rules cannot hope to make creative dramatists, but the dramatists of all ages have benefited much from the painstaking analysis which has been devoted to the work of their predecessors.

Weakness in the preparation of cinematic scripts may be due to a variety of causes, not least of which perhaps is the fact that many authors write for the screen with their left hand. They are interested in the money rather than sincerely moved to tell a story or express an idea.

But this cannot be taken alone. Perhaps Will Hays comes nearer to the truth when he says that

> Recognition of the motion pictures as an art by the great universities (will mark) the beginning of a new day in motion picture work. It (will pave) the way for the motion picture's Shakespeares.

This is no strained and fantastic statement. It means simply that through the aid of the detailed analysis and critical evaluation similar to that which the drama has been accorded, the ground will be prepared for surer mastery of effect; from the principles thus established the cinematic form of expression will be provided with that sense of purpose already attained by other arts of more extended ancestry. Shakespeare could not have been without the preparation made for him by the humanistic work of the academies; the "University wits," trained in the study of literature, were his immediate predecessors and masters.

For this the cinema is waiting.

www.ingramcontent.com/pod-product-compliance
Lightning Source LLC
LaVergne TN
LVHW090618110826
845146LV00001B/448

* 9 7 8 1 4 4 7 4 5 2 6 3 8 *